How Do You Know
It's Summer?

by Lisa M. Herrington

Content Consultant
Randy C. Bilik, M.A.
Julia A. Stark Elementary School, Stamford, Connecticut

Reading Consultant
Jeanne M. Clidas, Ph.D.
Reading Specialist

Children's Press®
An Imprint of Scholastic Inc.
New York Toronto London Auckland Sydney
Mexico City New Delhi Hong Kong
Danbury, Connecticut

Library of Congress Cataloging-in-Publication Data
Herrington, Lisa M., author.
How do you know it's summer? / by Lisa M. Herrington.
    pages cm. — (Rookie read-about science)
Summary: "Introduces the reader to the summer season."— Provided by publisher.
Audience: 3-6.
Includes index.
ISBN 978-0-531-29948-7 (library binding) — ISBN 978-0-531-22577-6 (pbk.)
1. Summer—Juvenile literature. I. Title. II. Title: How do you know it is summer?
III. Series: Rookie read-about science.
QB637.6.H474 2014
508.2—dc23   2013014928

Produced by Spooky Cheetah Press

© 2014 by Scholastic Inc.

Printed in China 62

SCHOLASTIC, CHILDREN'S PRESS, ROOKIE READ-ABOUT®, and associated logos
are trademarks and/or registered trademarks of Scholastic Inc.

1 2 3 4 5 6 7 8 9 10 R 23 22 21 20 19 18 17 16 15 14

Photographs © 2014: Adam Chinitz: 30; Alamy Images/Bill Brooks: 7; AP Images/
Mary Altaffer: 27, 31 top; Dreamstime/Dimitri Surkov: 16; Media Bakery: 24
(Ariel Skelley), 23 (Jose Luis Pelaez), 19 (Karine Aigner), cover (Kevin Dodge);
Shutterstock, Inc.: 3 top right (M. Unal Ozmen), 3 bottom (spaxiax); Superstock, Inc.:
8 (Belinda Images), 15, 31 center bottom (Burger/Phanie); Thinkstock: 4, 29 (Design
Pics), 3 top left, 11, 20, 31 center top, 31 bottom (iStockphoto), 28 (Purestock), 12 (Stock
Foundry/Design Pics).

Table of Contents

Welcome, Summer! 5

What's the Weather? 9

Plants and Animals in Summer 17

Kids in Summer 22

Let's Explore! 28

Let's Experiment! 30

Glossary 31

Index 32

Facts for Now 32

About the Author 32

Welcome, Summer!

The sun shines brightly.
Watermelons are ready to eat.
Fireflies light up the night sky.
That is how we know it is summer!

There are four seasons in each year. Each season lasts about three months. Summer is the season that comes after spring.

The first day of summer is usually June 20th or June 21st.

Winter

Spring

Summer

Fall

What's the Weather?

Summer is the hottest season. Most days are sunny. In summer, days last longer than at any other time of year. Sometimes it doesn't get dark until after bedtime!

FUN FACT!

The first day of summer has the most hours of daylight all year.

Boom! **Thunderstorms** are common in summer. They bring rain, wind, thunder, and lightning.

FUN FACT!

A lightning bolt is many times hotter than the sun. We hear a loud boom—thunder—when heat from lightning causes the air to expand.

It is hot out! We wear shorts, T-shirts, and sandals to stay cool. We put on our bathing suits to go swimming.

This girl is protecting herself from the sun.

The sun's rays are strong. Hats and **sunscreen** protect our skin from sunburn. Sunglasses keep our eyes safe from the sun.

To see the effects of the sun for yourself, try the experiment on page 30.

Plants and Animals in Summer

The sun helps plants and flowers grow. Trees are full of leaves. They give us shade from the hot sun.

This girl is reading a book beneath a shady tree.

Animals find food easily in summer. Deer **graze** on grass. Turtles eat bugs and small fish. Frogs catch insects on their tongues. *Ribbit!*

This bullfrog is waiting for its next meal to fly by!

This is a photo of a ruby-throated hummingbird.

Birds and insects are busy in summer. Bees, butterflies, and hummingbirds travel from flower to flower. They gather food and help spread seeds.

FUN FACT!

Hummingbirds can beat their tiny wings about 55 to 75 times a second. The flapping makes a humming sound.

Kids in Summer

In summer, there is no school. It is a great time to take a family trip. We hike, camp, fish, and swim. We build sand castles on the beach.

This boy and his dad are building a sand castle.

23

These kids are cheering for their Little League team.

Summer is a good time to be outdoors. We visit parks. We ride our bicycles. We cheer at baseball games.

Happy birthday, America! We celebrate the Fourth of July with picnics, cookouts, and parades. We watch colorful **fireworks** light up the sky.

FUN FACT!

On the Fourth of July, we remember how the United States gained its freedom from Great Britain a long time ago.

Let's Explore!

- Look at the picture. What do you see that tells you summer has arrived?

- Take a nature walk outside in summer. What clues can you find in your yard or neighborhood that say summer is here?

- In a science journal, draw pictures of what you observed. Write down some words that describe what you saw, heard, and smelled.

Food is a big part of summer. We grow vegetables in our garden. We pick berries. We set up lemonade stands. What is *your* favorite thing to do in summer?

Make a Sun Print

What You'll Need

- Colored construction paper
- Scissors
- A rock
- Sunshine

Directions

1. Place a piece of dark construction paper in a sunny spot. Ask an adult to help you use scissors to cut shapes from other pieces of paper.

2. Arrange the cutout shapes and the rock on the paper.

3. Leave the paper in the sun until the color fades.

4. Pull off the shapes and the rock. Notice that the areas underneath are dark.

Think About It: Why is it dark in the areas that were covered?

Answer: The sunlight faded the exposed areas of the paper. The areas that were protected from the sun stayed dark.

Glossary

fireworks (FIRE-wurks): devices that make loud noises and a display of colorful lights when they are burned or exploded

graze (grayz): to eat grass that is growing in a field

sunscreen (SUHN-skreen): a lotion that protects the skin from the sun's harmful rays

thunderstorms (THUHN-dur-storms): rainstorms with thunder and lightning

Index

animals 18

birds 21

clothes 13

flowers 17, 21

food 5, 18, 21, 29

Fourth of July 26

insects 5, 18, 21

rain 10

seasons 6

summer activities
22–29

sun 5, 9, 14, 17

thunderstorms 10

trees 17

weather 9–14

Facts for Now

Visit this Scholastic Web site for more information on summer:
www.factsfornow.scholastic.com
Enter the keyword **Summer**

About the Author

Lisa M. Herrington is a freelance writer and editor. She lives in
Trumbull, Connecticut, with her husband, Ryan, and her daughter,
Caroline. Her favorite parts of summer include swimming in her pool,
collecting shells on the beach, and eating fresh corn on the cob.